Seasons

What Can You See in Spring?

Siân Smith

Heinemann
LIBRARY

Chicago, Illinois

© 2015 Heinemann Library
an imprint of Capstone Global Library, LLC
Chicago, Illinois

Edited by James Benefield and Kathryn Clay
Designed by Richard Parker
Picture research by Tracy Cummins
Production by Helen McCreath
Originated by Capstone Global Library Ltd
Printed in the United States of America in
Eau Claire, Wisconsin. 113017 010961RP

Library of Congress Cataloging-in-Publication Data
Cataloging-in-publication information is on file
with the Library of Congress.
ISBN 978-1-4846-0354-3 (paperback)
ISBN 978-1-4846-0365-9 (eBook PDF)

Photo Credits

Dreamstime.com: © Hupeng, 11, 22; iStockphoto: © aimintang, 7, © coramueller, 16, back cover, © Madzia71, 8, © Milan Zeremski, 15; Shutterstock: Algefoto, 17, Anne Kitzman, 9, ayosphoto, 20 middle, Drew Rawcliffe, 13, Franck Boston, 20 left, LittleStocker, 6, Matej Kastelic, 4, 22, Ozerov Alexander, 18, Pavel L Photo and Video, 20 right, Peter Wey, front cover, Phant, 12, Richard Schramm, 21, Rtimages, 19, Simon Greig, 5, Smit, 14, Vlasta Kaspar, 10

Contents

Things You Can See
in Spring. 4

Spring Quiz 20

Picture Glossary. 22

Index 22

Notes for Teachers
and Parents 23

In This Book 24

Things You Can See in Spring

buds

You can see **buds**.

You can see daffodils.

You can see tulips.

blossoms

You can see blossoms.

bee

You can see bees.

nest

You can see nests.

You can see ducklings.

You can see **tadpoles**.

You can see piglets.

You can see lambs.

You can see rain.

You can see umbrellas.

You can see rain boots.

puddle

You can see puddles.

You can see rainbows.

You can see kites.

Spring Quiz

Which clothes would you wear in spring?

The four seasons follow a pattern. Which season comes after spring?

spring

?

winter

fall

Picture Glossary

 **bud**

 **tadpole**

Index

bee, 8
blossom, 7
bud, 4

daffodil, 5
duckling, 10

kite, 19

lamb, 13

nest, 9

piglet, 12
puddle, 17

rain, 14
rain boot, 16
rainbow, 18

tadpole, 11
tulip, 6

umbrella, 15

Answer to quiz on page 20: rain coat
Answer to question on page 21: summer

Notes for Teachers and Parents

Before Reading

Building background: Talk about the seasons of the year. Which season are we in at the moment? Ask children what they would see if they looked out a window in spring.

After Reading

Recall and reflect: Which season is before spring? Which season follows spring? What is the weather like in spring? What is the best thing about spring?

Sentence knowledge: Help children count the number of words in each sentence.

Word knowledge (phonics): Look at the word *see* on any page. Ask the child to think of words that rhyme with *see*. (bee, sea, he, me, knee, tea)

Word recognition: Have children point to the word *see* on page 5. Ask children to find the word *see* on other pages.

Extending Ideas

Grow Eggshell Heads: Give each child an empty eggshell with the top cut off. Curl a piece of pipe cleaner to make a base, and stick it to the bottom of the eggshell. Draw a face on the eggshell. Put some potting soil in the eggshell, and then sprinkle in some grass seeds. Cover the seeds with more soil and water lightly. (It may take 10 days for the seeds to germinate.) When the seeds begin to sprout, put the eggshell heads on a sunny window ledge.

In This Book

Topic Words
bees
blossoms
buds
daffodils
ducklings
kites
lambs
nests
piglets
puddles
rain
rain boots
rainbows
tadpoles
tulips
umbrellas

Topic
Spring

High-frequency Words
a
can
see
you

Sentence Stem
You can see _____.

Ask Children to Read These Words:

buds	p. 4
daffodils	p. 5
nests	p. 9
ducklings	p. 10
piglets	p. 12